Climate Change *and the* Great Plagues

A Brief History of Climate-Driven Bubonic Plague Pandemics

R. CHRISTIAN BILICH

First paperback edition March 2021

ISBN 978-1-7368706-0-0 (Paperback)
ISBN 978-1-7368706-1-7 (E-Book)

Published by Istari Press
www.istaripress.com

Table of Contents

Abstract

The two great bubonic plague outbreaks of history, Justinian's Plague and the Black Death were responsible for the deaths of over one hundred million individuals across Eurasia and Africa. Both occurrences of the plague coincided with climatic shifts that are well documented by both literary and physical evidence. This brief history explores the possibility that both Justinian's Plague and the Black Death were precipitated by climatic shifts preceding their respective eras and that these changes also contributed to disappearance of each pandemic. A scientific analysis investigating the climatic changes including the anomalous weather of 535-536 A.D., the Medieval Warm Period, and the Little Ice Age are correlated with literary evidence recording the transmission and dormancy sequence of the plague. Although distinct differences exist between the origins of climate change in the periods preceding each plague, the effects of such changes clearly resulted in conditions ideal for the resulting pandemics.

Preface

Climate Change and the Great Plagues began as academic research by the author in late 2007. The author conjoined keen interest in Medieval / Byzantine studies and environmental science in order to offer a possible explanation for the two greatest mortality events in recorded history, the bubonic plague outbreak known as Justinian's Plague and infamous Black Death. Much of our contemporary world was indelibly shaped by these two events. In the case of the former, the plague represented the high water mark of the Eastern Roman Empire that would decline in no small part due to population loss associated with the pandemic. This would ultimately pave the way for the Arab conquests and the separate development of Western Europe. In the case of the Black Death, the socio-economic of structure of Europe was irretrievably changed. Europe experienced the greatest economic depression in its history, major cities were abandoned, and feudalism began to crumble due to labor shortages. The realities eventually gave rise to the Renaissance and the age of exploration / colonization.

In the present day, as the world is beset by the Covid-19 global pandemic, the author feels compelled to publish this work as a stark reminder that the vicissitudes the global population are enduring are not new to humanity. Pandemics, by their very nature, rend the societal bonds that allow complex nation states to thrive socially, economically, and even militarily. Understanding the genesis of pandemic-scale pestilence is of particular concern to every society and potential mitigation strategies to avoid mass outbreaks are therefore of critical importance. *Climate Change and the Great Plagues* attempts to make the case through a historical lens that environmental factors beyond human control were responsible for the two greatest pandemics in recorded history. With that being said, the historical context afforded the reader might lead to a greater understanding of zoonotic spillover pandemic events and the foundational climatic triggers which drive disease propagation and regression cycles.

Introduction

"During these times there was a pestilence, by which the whole human race came near to being annihilated. Now in the case of all other scourges sent from heaven some explanation of a cause might be given by daring men, such as the many theories propounded by those who are clever in these matters, for they love to conjure up causes which are absolutely incomprehensible to man...But for this calamity, it is quite impossible either to express in words or to conceive in thought any explanation, except indeed to refer it to God.

- Procopius, *History of the Wars*, II, xxii

"Climate change will have wide-ranging and mostly damaging impacts on human health. There have been periods of uncontrollable waves of disease that radically altered human civilization in the past, such as when Europe's population was devastated by bubonic plague in the Middle Ages. Now a warming climate, compounded by widespread ecological changes, may be stimulating wide-scale changes in disease patterns"

- Dr Paul Epstein of the Centre for Health and Global Environment

Modern society is quite familiar with epidemic disease. In this age various forms of media relay constant information deemed essential to public health and warn of deadly outbreaks of Covid-19, SARS, Avian Influenza, and Ebola. These terrifying diseases force humanity to confront the grim reality that microscopic bacteria and viruses continue to hold sway over the human condition and can alter an entire society in a matter of weeks. Although modern medicine has tended to give humanity a false sense of security, epidemic diseases have in the past and will continue to alter the lives of human beings. Although the diseases mentioned above have certainly taken many lives and affected the human condition in the modern era, their impact pales in comparison to the two greatest pandemics ever experienced by man, Justinian's Plague and the Black Death. Together these pandemics were responsible for the death of at least one hundred million people, toppled several established civilizations, and terrorized mankind for centuries before vanishing almost as quickly as it had originated. The biological identity of the plague and its transmission vectors were a medical mystery until the 20th century and the causes behind its prolific spread during both pandemics have never been fully explained.

The Bubonic or Black plague has been a significant natural selective force on human populations throughout the last two millennia of recorded history. It seems likely that *Yersinia pestis,* the bacteria responsible for the plague, has been associated with the human condition on some level since the rise of agriculture and the subsequent domestication of animals. In fact, plague expert Charles Gregg believes that plague may have affected *Homo erectus* as proto- humans began hunting plague-ridden game that made for a tempting and easy meal. Gregg believes the disease did not become epidemic until the rise of agriculture brought about large human settlements which disrupted natural rodent populations where the plague is endemic.[1] Reservoirs of the plague are common amongst rodent populations in Asia and Africa, where natural hosts such as the gerbil carry the *Yersinia pestis* bacillus, yet are immune to it. Occasionally environmental exigencies will

---

1 Karlen, Arno. *Man and Microbe,* (New York: Simon & Schuster, 1995), 24.

necessitate these wild rodents coming into to close proximity to human beings and their livestock.[2] Plague outbreaks appear to be related to increased abundance of rodents and other mammals that serve as hosts for the fleas that then transmit the disease to humans.[3] A search for the first link in the chain of causation that precipitated the two great bubonic plague pandemics, Justinian's Plague (542AD-750AD) and the Black Death (1347AD-early 1700'sAD) must begin with isolating occurrences that led to large scale interaction between human communities and foraging rodent populations hosting the *Xenopsylla cheopis* flea carrying the Yersinia bacillus. These fleas, the vectors of plague transmission, actually get sick and die of the plague and it is in the process of the fleas dying that the plague cleverly jumps from host to host. A fibrin clot forms in the stomach of the flea by multiplying Yersinia Pestis bacteria and starve the flea to death due to shut down in digestion. In a climatic correlation, the fibrin clot only forms at temperatures below 77 degrees Fahrenheit. Above this threshold the clot does not form and the plague bacillus is simply passed out of the flea with the feces.[4] It is only at the ideal temperature that the clot will form and the ravenous flea will then jump onto anything that moves, irrespective of whether or not it is a natural host. The dying flea will be unable to satiate its hunger and so it will continue to move from host to host, vainly hoping to quell its hunger until it dies. In this way the plague actually produces the mechanism for its own spread.[5] Compounding the problem, the same moist climate conditions may act to promote flea survival and reproduction, also enhancing plague transmission.[6]

---

[2] Keys, David. *Catastrophe* (New York: Ballantine Books, 1999), 63.

[3] Parmenter, Robert. As quoted in "Human Plague Cases Increasing in Southwest." National Science Foundation Press Release. NSF PR 99-70 - November 19, 1999. http://www.nsf.gov/od/lpa/news/press/99/pr9970.htm; Accessed May 2, 2007

[4] Kavenaugh, Dan. "Specific Effect of Temperature Upon Transmission of the Plague Bacillus by the Oriental RatFlea, *Xenopsylla Cheopis*" *The American Journal of Tropical Medicine and Hygiene Vol. 20* (1971): 264-273

[5] Keys, *Catastrophe*, 270.

[6] Ibid., 19-20

The next link in the transmission chain is related to the relative abundance of secondary hosts for the plague bacillus. It seems intuitive that increased precipitation enhances small mammal food resources such as plants and insects, leading to a population explosion where competition for such resources quickly surpasses a sustainable level. Consequently, the rodents must increase their cumulative range in order to survive, bringing them in contact with normally plague free rodents which live in close proximity to man.[7] Another possibility that would theoretically yield the same result is a drought scenario followed by excessive rainfall, whereby both rodents and their predators die off in massive numbers. The faster breeding rodent population recovers quicker and leads to a predator/prey imbalance and a resultant population explosion and the afore-mentioned transmission sequence.

In either scenario, the weather drives the motor that invariably brings native plague-carrying but plague-resistant mammals such as gerbils and multimammate mice into contact with *Rattus rattus*, or black rat, a species that specializes in infesting human environments such as farms, storehouses, markets, and ships.[8]

The Plague of Justinian and The Black Death combined were responsible for the estimated deaths of between 100 million and 150 million individuals, representing between 25%-40% of the then extant populations of Eurasia and Africa.[9] Isolating the climatic vicissitudes that gave raise to such devastating mortality in the past can serve as a caveat to present and future generations as the present generation becomes cognizant of the massive affect that climate has on nearly every conceivable facet of human existence. Fortunately, there are a number of primary sources available from each epoch that reveal the prevailing climate and weather anomalies that immediately preceded each pandemic. Additionally, the modern

---

7 Ibid.

8 Ibid.; 21

9 Ruddiman, William. *Plows, Plagues, and Petroleum*, (Princeton: Princeton University Press, 2005), 134-135.

researcher is aided by a host of emergent fields such as dendrochronology, climatology, volcanology, epidemiology/genetics, and astrophysics with which to help complete the climatic puzzle that precipitated the two greatest natural calamities in human history. It is hoped that this knowledge will aid humanity in understanding more fully the inextricable link between global climate change and pandemic disease occurrences. Although much has been learned about climate as it relates to pathogenesis, identifying the exact correlation between the two historically is fertile ground for new research.

A voluminous amount of research has been conducted on the Black Death. Such research is primarily comprised of Eurocentric material focused on the plague's socio-economic impact during its initial outbreak in the late fourteenth century. Much less has been written about Justinian's Plague, with nearly all available sources cited in this work. The vast majority of these have been written within the past ten years, representing an emerging sub-field within Roman-Byzantine studies, environmental history, as well as several scientific fields listed above. The present body of scholarly work investigating possible climatic causes for the occurrence of the plague pandemics is almost non-existent. One of the few contemporary works that has made such an argument is Davis Keys' *Catastrophe.* Keys draws from an eclectic array of literary sources and cites the work of several well-known scientists who have found corroborating scientific evidence for an abrupt climate change immediately preceding the first plague pandemic. This history will explore the compelling evidence that climatic change brought on by natural volcanism contributed to ideal environmental conditions for the pandemic known as Justinian's Plague. Additionally, the correlation between global climate shifts and the Black Death will be explored. Comparisons as well as disparities between Justinian's Plague and the Black Death will be analyzed in order to determine how climate affected both the genesis as well as disappearance of both pandemics. The conclusion drawn will offer evidence to support a new research in a field of study that has been mostly unexplored.

The Climate Anomaly of 535AD – 536AD

The evidence for catastrophic climate change occurring in 535AD is ubiquitous and compelling. The event was witnessed on four continents and all accounts generally speak of the dimming of the sun for approximately eighteen months with resultant crop failures,

Vesuvius from Portici by Joseph Wright of Derby (1776)

famine, and migrations ensuing.[10] Procopius, the court historian for the Emperor Justinian and our best primary source of the period, writing from Constantinople in early 536AD, states "during this year a most dread portent took place. For the sun gave forth its light without brightness ... and it seemed exceedingly like the sun in eclipse, for the beams it shed were not clear."[11] Writing one thousand miles away in the Italy of King Theodoric, praetorian prefect Cassiodorus wrote to a subordinate: "The sun ... seems to have lost its wonted light, and appears of a bluish color. We marvel to see no shadows of our bodies at noon, to feel the mighty vigor of the sun's heat wasted into feebleness, and the phenomena which accompany an eclipse prolonged through almost a whole year. We have had ... a summer without heat ... the crops have been chilled by north winds... the rain is denied ..."[12] Almost five thousand miles away in China, an unnamed chronicler in the *Nan shi* or *The History of the Southern Dynasties* recorded an entry in November 535AD that "yellow dust rained down like snow and could be scooped up by the handfuls." Further entries catalog anomalous weather between May 535AD and September 536AD, "because of drought there was an imperial edict which ordered the wholesale burial of corpses in mass graves.... provide amnesty from rents and taxes....and send special inspectors to investigate armies of famished refugees who were wandering aimlessly north of the Yellow River."[13] Further entries speak of "great hail storms....and in Shaanxi province mortality of 80% as people resorted to cannibalism due to famine."[14]

---

[10] Keys, *Catastrophe*, 3.

[11] From: Procopius, *History of the Wars*, 7 Vols. trans. H. B. Dewing, Loeb Library of the Greek and Roman Classics, (Cambridge, Mass.: Harvard University Press, 1914), Vol. I, pp. 451-473

[12] Linden, Eugene. *The Winds of Change: Climate, Weather, and the Destruction of Civilizations.* (New York: Simon & Schuster, 2006), 57. [translated letter of Cassiodorus]

[13] Keys, *Catastrophe*, 153.

[14] Ibid., 153.

Thousands of miles away, the climatic events of the period certainly affected the Americas, although with the exception of the Maya written records are sparse. Tree ring analysis, or dendrochronology, utilizes growth rings to decipher the prevailing climatic patterns in a given area.[15] Analysis of the rings of the bristlecone pine, the oldest living organism on Earth, clearly show evidence of a deteriorating climate of colder and drier weather beginning in the mid 530's and lasting approximately 20 years.[16] Further evidence of climatic cooling occurring in the mid sixth century in the Americas comes via ice core samples from Andean glaciers that reveal that the period was the driest in a 3300-year-long sequence.[17] Mayan ciphers from Tikal also speak of prolonged drought in the period corresponding to the mid sixth century. This fact is also corroborated by climatologists' analysis of the oxygen-18 isotope in mollusk shells which were extracted in sediment from dry lakes throughout Mesoamerica.[18] Elsewhere, the great trading kingdom of Marib (modern Yemen) began to depopulate due to chronic drought followed by massive flooding, which undermined its legendary dam several times during the mid to late 530's and led to widespread famine across the Arabian Peninsula.[19] The Arab poet, Matrud, as quoted by the ninth century Arab historian al-Tabari, chronicled a Meccan famine in the mid sixth century. Amr, the great grandfather of Muhammad, "broke bread for tharid (broth) for his people when the men of Mecca were drought-stricken and lean."[20] Clearly there is a preponderance of physical and literary evidence pointing to a massive climatic shift worldwide in the mid 530's, with Eurasia being the likely locus. The obvious question is what kind of event could trigger worldwide climate fluctuations of the

---

[15] Diamond, Jared. *Collapse: How Societies Choose to Fail or Succeed.* (New York: Penguin Books, 2005), 138.

[16] Keys, *Catastrophe*, 189.

[17] Ibid.; 191

[18] Diamond, *Collapse*, 173.

[19] Keys, *Catastrophe*, 63.

[20] El Cheikh, Nadia Maria, *Byzantium as Viewed by the Arabs*, (Cambridge: Cambridge University Press, 2004), 8.

magnitude of the above-referenced accounts? Still another question, more germane to research concerning the immediate climatic antecedents of the Plague of Justinian is whether the chronological correlation between these anomalies and the plague represent de facto causation.

Probable Causes of Climate Event and Incidence of Justinian's Plague

What caused the great geophysical calamity of 535-536, as evidenced in tree-ring measurements, ice cores, sediment analysis, and human records of the period? There are three

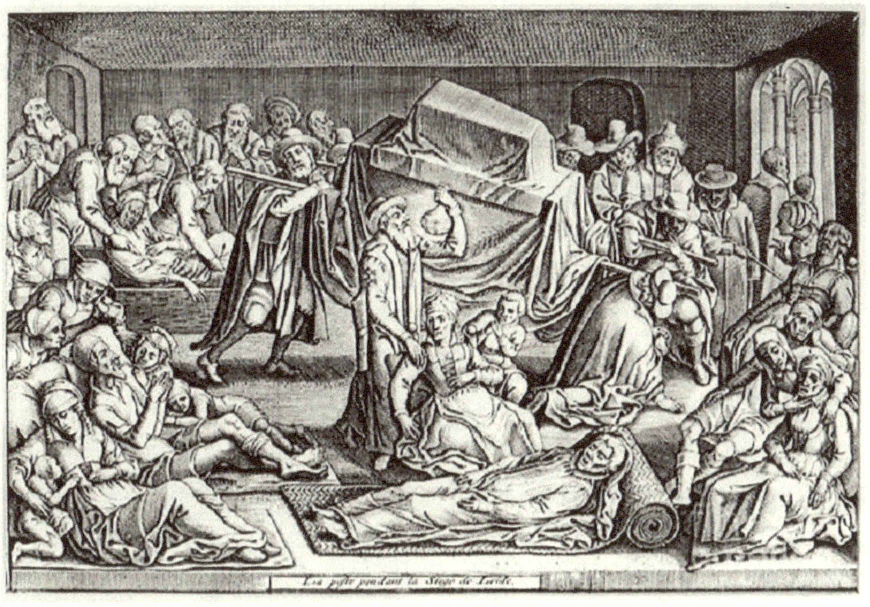

Plague in Leiden The Netherlands During The Spanish Siege Of 1574 by J. Orlers (1614)

plausible explanations: a comet or asteroid impact, ocean current conveyer disruption, or a massive volcanic / super-volcanic event. The impact event popularized by dendrochronology expert Mike Baillie has not been accepted by mainstream research scientists due to a couple of inconsistencies. First, a discernable impact crater dating from the period has never been found on land, even in the age of 3-D satellite imagery. Other compelling geological markers of an impact event such as an iridium layer dating from the period have never been found in the geological record. Even a deep ocean impact event would have left a tell-tale crater which would not have been eroded within fifteen hundred years. Additionally, literary and archaeological evidence show no record of the massive tidal wave an ocean impact would have produced.[21] The absence of an impact crater and other geologic indicators coupled with a lack of literary and archeological evidence of a resultant massive tsunami makes proof of an asteroid or comet collision hypothesis tenuous.

Oceanic current disruption described and cited in a later section of this paper as a possible contributor to the Little Ice Age, is a known factor of sudden climate change. The engine of this global conveyer of ocean currents is the Gulf Stream current that brings warm water north from the tropics. At around 40° North – the latitude of Portugal and New York – the current divides. Some water heads southwards in a surface current while the rest continues north, leading to warming winds that are known to raise European temperatures by 5°C to 10°C.[22] These winds are the result of an atmospheric tug-of-war, a phenomenon known as the North Atlantic Current Oscillation. This phenomenon is noted in detail below, but is not generally accepted as the culprit behind the climatic event of 535-536 for a variety of reasons. Current disruption can explain the cold weather, retarded tree growth, as well as droughts and floods. Current disruptions, however, fail to account for three crucial pieces of evidence

---

[21] Keys, *Catastrophe*, 241-243.

[22] Pearce, Fred. "Failing Ocean Current Raises Fears of a Mini Ice Age." NewScientist.com. November 30, 2005. http://www.newscientist.com/article.ns?id=dn8398;

from the period. First, current alone cannot explain the pervasive darkness of the sky or the bluish tint of the sun described by contemporary sources, including Cassiodorus and Procopius. Secondly, current fluctuations in the Atlantic can have global effects much like El Nino events in the Pacific, but the presence of falling ash cited in Chinese imperial court records seem to suggest an eruption event. Lastly, ice core samples record voluminous amounts of sulphuric acid from the period, corroborating the Chinese observations.

In light of these considerations, some scholars, most notably David Keys, favor volcanism as the cause of the climate anomalies that occurred in the mid sixth century. It is highly probable, however, that Keys relied heavily on the work of Yale historian Ellsworth Huntington, who hypothesized that massive volcanic eruptions in the Indonesian arc could possibly be responsible for worldwide climatic shifts and perhaps even disease occurrences. Although Marcus Linden clearly noted the correlation, Keys himself never cites Huntington's seminal 1919 work, *The Pulse of Asia: A Journey in Central Asia Illustrating the Geographic Basis of History*.[23] Although Huntington intuitively conjectured that volcanism was a major climatic driver that has had tremendous effects on human history, the scientific technology to verify such claims was not available in his era. The most compelling scientific evidence for an eruption event involves the discovery of sulfuric acid of volcanic origin in ice cores from both the north and south poles within the strata associated with the ten-year period from 535 to 545.

This is important because for the ash fallout, or "dry fog" to be found on both poles, is indicative of an eruption in the tropics which further

---

[23] Linden, *The Winds of Change*, 61. [Keys drew inferences from earlier work by Yale historian, Ellsworth Huntington in his work *The Pulse of Asia: A Journey in Central Asia Illustrating the Geographic Basis of History* (Houghton Mifflin, 1919)]

narrows the possible culprits.[24] The fact that sulphuric acid/snow deposition took place at least twice as long in Antarctica as in Greenland suggests that the eruption in question occurred in the southern rather than the northern tropics.[25] Dry fogs spawned by large volcanic eruptions cool the climate by partially blocking incident sunlight and perturbing atmospheric circulation patterns.[26] Although the effects of volcanic winter are well-known, did volcanically-induced climatic cooling cause the widespread crop failures that preceded the pandemic and ultimately create conditions ideal for Justinian's Plague a full five years later? It is clear from the dendrochronological record and from contemporary sources that the temperature dropped, and without the full strength of the sun to heat and evaporate the oceans' surfaces, there would have been less moisture released into the atmosphere. As a result, there would have been colder temperatures and progressively less rainfall worldwide resulting in drought and shortly thereafter, famine.

Richard Stothers, a scientist with NASA's Goddard Institute for Space Studies, has spent decades reading ancient manuscripts in search of evidence linking volcanoes to sudden climate change. By comparing the dates of past eruption events with historical accounts of atmospheric phenomena, Stothers has found compelling evidence that large eruptions can significantly alter global climate and can even cause crop failures and disease pandemics worldwide.[27] Strothers observes,

> Bitterly cold winters followed the great Mediterranean dry fogs and famine became locally widespread, aggravated or caused by poor harvests following the chilly, rain-deprived

---

[24] Stothers, Richard. *Volcanic Dry Fogs, Climate Cooling, and Plague Pandemics in Europe and the Middle East.* October 20, 1998. NASA Climate Research Program. http://pubs.giss.nasa.gov/abstracts/1999/Stothers_4.html

[25] Keys, *Catastrophe*, 249.

[26] Ibid.; 250.

[27] "The Volcano and Climate Model" Earth Bulletins. April 2007. The American Museum of Natural History Accessed via <http://earthbulletin.amnh.org/D/3/2/

> summers that accompanied the dry fogs. Severe famine can lead to disease in both animals and humans due to lowered body resistance, creating a feedback loop that virtually ceases the agricultural output of food producers. It is this scenario that causes the association of famine with the great pandemics, especially in those regions with endemic plague, such as central Asia and northeastern Africa.[28]

Since known reservoirs of plague occur in northeastern Africa, then a certain measure of validity must be given to Procopius' account of the origins of the first pandemic. He states "It started from the Egyptians who dwell in Pelusium. Then it divided and moved in one direction towards Alexandria and the rest of Egypt, and in the other direction it came to Palestine on the borders of Egypt; and from there it spread over the whole world, always moving forward and traveling at times favorable to it."[29]

It should be expected that a large tropical eruption in 535 would yield unseasonable weather and that crop failures and resultant famines would naturally occur after some lag time, so it is not surprising that the first instance of the plague in Lower Egypt occurred five years after a volcanic event darkened the sky. Due to the fact that the primary vectors of the plague bacillus are *Rattus rattus* and *Xenopsylla cheopis,* the plague followed a favorable proliferation route along military and commercial trade routes that had been heavily utilized for five centuries.[30] The speed at which the plague spread along such routes would have been astonishing. Given that Egypt had been wracked with famine for five years, the plague spread like wild fire through a weakened populace. Most ships that left Egypt, the

---

[28] Stothers, Richard. *Volcanic Dry Fogs, Climate Cooling, and Plague Pandemics in Europe and the Middle East.* http://pubs.giss.nasa.gov/abstracts/1999/Stothers_4.html

[29] From: Procopius, *History of the Wars*, 7 Vols. trans. H. B. Dewing, Loeb Library of the Greek and Roman Classics, (Cambridge, Mass.: Harvard University Press, 1914), Vol. I, 451-473

[30] Ibid.

breadbasket of the late Roman Empire, were exporting grain to the world's largest and most powerful city at that time, Constantinople. [31]It was just a few weeks until opportunistic rats and their ravenous parasitic fleas in their billions would set sail to decimate the known world.

There is strong physical evidence of climate disaster brought on by the "dry fog" volcanic winter effect usually associated with volcanism or more rarely cosmic impact events. The period of 535-536 saw unseasonably cold temperatures resulting from the sun being effectively blotted out and plant life experienced stunted growth as evidenced from tree rings analysis. According to tree ring research presented in 2001 by dendrochronology expert Markus Lindholm, the "most dramatic shift in growing conditions, from favorable to unfavorable, between two years, took place between A.D. 535-536" in Europe and Africa. Lindholm's findings were corroborated by Mike Baillie, who utilized trees encased in peat bogs, stated "It was a catastrophic environmental downturn that shows up in trees all over the world. Temperatures dropped enough to hinder the growth of trees as widely dispersed as northern Europe, Siberia, western North America, and southern South America."[32]

There is no supporting evidence for an impact-related event, leaving the assumption by Keys (vis-à-vis Huntington), Linden, Stothers, and others of a volcanic eruption as the strongest probable candidate. The

---

[31] Little, Lester. *Plague and the End of Antiquity: The Pandemic of 541-750* (Cambridge: Cambridge University Press, 2007), 3.

Markus Lindholm, et al. "Interannual and decade scale changes in northern Fennoscandian midsummer temperatures since 5500 B.C. extracted from the supra-long ring-width chronology of Scots pine" {Abstract} 23 July 2001. http://www.wsl.ch/forest/dendro2001/abstracts/abs110.ehtml [cited by William Sutherland "Days of Darkness (AD 535-AD 546)" Accessed via < http://ezinearticles.com/?Days-of-Darkness-(AD-535-AD-546)&id=202540

[32] Sutherand, William. "Days of Darkness (AD 535-AD 546)". May 21, 2006. http://ezinearticles.com/Days-of-Darkness-(AD-535-AD-546) &id=202540. [Sutherland cited Baille, "Catastrophic event preceded Dark Ages – scientist" Reuters. September 8, 2000. http://www.freerepublic.com/forum/a39b91ca42b27.htm]

case for eruption related climate change is validated nicely by the ubiquity of sulphuric acid in ice cores sampled in Greenland, Antarctica, and even in the Andes. The prevalence of volcanic materials within ice cores worldwide points to an eruption in the tropical zone, most probably in the Indonesian arc. The eruption affected both hemispheres and brought about several decades of disrupted climate patterns, most notably colder and drier weather in Europe and Asia, where descriptions of months with diminished sun light, persistent cold and anomalous summer snow falls are recorded in 6th-century written accounts. The literary records also speak of massive floods in Africa and Arabia, ash fallout in China, and famine world-wide resulting from the inability to sustain crop yields in the face of unfavorable weather.[33]

Ultimately, the cold rainy weather, or more probably droughts followed by such weather, brought about a population explosion among endemic Yersinia carriers such as the African gerbil. These rodents were forced out from their normally enclosed ecosystem in northeastern Africa in an effort to feed their ever-increasing numbers. This brought them into contact with the *Rattus rattus*, a rodent that has evolved into an almost symbiotic relationship with human beings. The parasitic hitchhiker, *Xenopsylla cheopis*, unable to feed itself due to the *Yersinia pestis* bacillus, jumped desperately from rat to human at a frenetic pace. Procopius' account of the outbreak originating at Peluseum provides the final clue to the transmission lines upon which Justinian's plague took; traveling along well established military and trading routes. Peluseum lies within a few hundred miles from the natural range of the plague-carrying African gerbil, so the five years of elapsed time between the probable eruption in Indonesia, resultant climate vicissitudes, and the ultimate outbreak of the plague seem reasonable considering the events and the logistics involved.

---

[33] Ruddiman, *Plows, Plagues, and Petroleum*, 139.

The Disappearance of the Plague – The Medieval Warm Period

In a total of 210 years spanning 541-750, there were about eighteen recorded outbreaks of the plague, ranging from Ireland to Persia and Scandinavia to southern Africa. The plague probably visited China and Southeast Asia as well, although surviving sources from these areas

Peasants before an Inn by Jan Steen (1654)

are virtually non-existent.[34] Around 750 the plague suddenly disappears from literature of the period and so we are led to believe that it probably retreated to its endemic reservoirs in Asia and Africa. [35]The factors behind the plague's disappearance are a mystery to historians as well as scientists. Did a series of events similar to the incipient pathogenesis of the plague occur to hasten its demise? Previously presented literary and physical evidence make the case for volcanism being directly responsible for the climate anomalies of 535-536 that created conditions ideal for the Justinian's Plague pandemic. Therefore, if climate created optimal conditions for the plague then it is reasonable to assume that climatic conditions less favorable to plague transmission and proliferation probably halted its spread.

The disappearance of Justinian's plague coincides with an epoch known as the Medieval Warm Period (MWP). This was a time of unusually warm climate in Eurasia lasting from about 800 until 1300 A.D., and roughly correlates with a time of high solar activity called the Medieval Maximum.[36] Although the relationship between solar activity and abrupt climate change is not well understood, a strong correlation seems to exist between major climate shifts and carbon-14 levels within tree rings, perhaps indicating long-term changes in solar radiation may have profound effects on terrestrial climate.[37] Climatic reconstruction of this era from climate proxies such as tree ring samples, atmospheric CO^2 contained within ice cores, and even coral isotopes indicate surface temperatures that averaged 1-2 degrees centigrade higher than today.[38] Additional anecdotal evidence is inferred from accounts of grapes growing in England, the founding of

---

[34] Little, *Plague and the End of Antiquity*, 116-119.

[35] Linden, *The Winds of Change*, 60.

[36] Fagan, Brian. *The Little Ice Age: How Climate Made History*. (New York: Basic Books, 2000), 47.

[37] Fagan, Brian. *The Long Summer: How Climate Changed Civilization*. (New York: Basic Books, 2004), 198.

[38] Houghton, J. T. et al, (eds) 2001, *Climate Change 2001: The Scientific Basis*, Intergovernmental Panel on Climate Change (IPCC), Cambridge University Press, Cambridge, UK. www.grida.no/climate/ipcc_tar/wg1/070.htm

the Norse settlement of Greenland due to an ice-free North Atlantic, as well as higher tree lines witnessed in the Alps.[39] It is highly probable that given the previously mentioned correlation between cool wet weather and incidence of *Yersinia pestis* contagion during 541-750 outbreaks that the MWP was a major contributing factor in the disappearance of Justinian's plague. Other contributing factors mentioned by William McNeil include endemic or acquired biological immunity and a smaller population that had become more rural than urban in nature after the initial waves of the plague had passed.[40] Whatever the causes, Justinian's Plague would be the last recorded bubonic plague pandemic for nearly six centuries, although small, localized outbreaks after 750 are recorded in the coastal provinces of China.[41] The next wave of bubonic plague, The Black Death, so named for hallmark black skin resulting from the septicemic form of bubonic plague, would come from an Asian, not African bacillus reservoir and travel with the conquering Mongol hordes across Eurasia.

Were climatic fluctuations again responsible for the swiftness by which *Yersinia Pestis* proliferated out from its natural loci to decimate the world of humanity once again?

---

[39] Fagan, *The Long Summer*, 247. & Diamond, *Collapse*, 181.

[40] McNeil, *Plagues and People*, 142-144.

[41] Ibid., 150-151.

The Little Ice Age

The Little Ice Age (LIA) was a period of climatic cooling that occurred after five centuries of the Medieval Warm Period. Climatologists and historians find it difficult to agree on either the start or end dates of this period, but many researchers generally regard the LIA as spanning from the late 13th to 17th centuries.[42] It was initially believed that the LIA was a global phenomenon, although it is now less clear if this is true. The Intergovernmental Panel on Climate Change

A Scene on Ice by Hendrick Avercamp (1625)

[42] Lamb, H.H. *Climate. History, and the Modern World.* (London: Routledge, 1995),195.

(IPCC) describes the LIA as a modest cooling of the Northern Hemisphere during this period of approximately 1°C, and says current evidence does not support globally synchronous periods of anomalous cold over this timeframe associated with it.[43] The IPCC utilized a myriad of proxies, or geophysical evidence, worldwide to deduce this finding, yet more localized proxies can be utilized to draw inferences of anomalous climate shifts that occurred in particular areas of interest; in this case Eurasia. Physical evidence of LIA-induced climate changes in Eurasia is crucial to understanding any link between such changes and the incidence of the Black Death of 1347. In order to extrapolate the prevailing climate of the LIA, climatologists and historians utilize ice core samples, tree ring and botanical data, as well as contemporary accounts contained within crop records, literature, and art.

The Evidence

Data from the Greenland ice core GISP-2, which is extracted by measuring the ratio of O^{18} vs. O^{16} (oxygen) isotopes that indicates the temperature of the snow at the time it was formed, was used to quantify the ambient temperatures of the period.[44] This ice core and others like it from glaciers in the Himalayas, Alps, and Scandinavia concur that the period 1308-1362 saw the coolest temperatures on record for the previous one thousand years.[45] These dates are corroborated by cores retrieved from glacial peat deposits at the northeastern edge of the Qinghai-Tibetan Plateau of China. On the basis of power spectrum analyses of O^{18} variations, the researchers further concluded that the "main driving force" of

[43] Houghton, J. T. et al, (eds) 2001, *Climate Change 2001: The Scientific Basis*, Intergovernmental Panel on Climate Change (IPCC), Cambridge University Press, Cambridge, UK. www.grida.no/climate/ipcc_tar/wg1/070.htm;

[44] Fagan *The Little Ice Age: How Climate Made History*. (New York: Basic Books, 2005), 66.

[45] Ibid., 66-67.

the changing climate that produced the Little Ice Age's three ultra-cold episodes, including the circa 1308-1362 span, was obtained "from solar activities."[46] A study in Russia developed a proxy temperature record based on tree- ring data obtained from the cores of 118 ice-encased trees that grew near the upper timberline in Siberia over the period 212 BC to AD 1996. This record agreed well with air temperature variations reconstructed from Greenland and Himalayan ice core data, suggesting to them that "the tree ring chronology of [the Siberian] region can be used to analyze both regional peculiarities as well as temperature variations in the Northern Hemisphere."[47] Further botanical evidence suggesting a climatic shift to a colder time in the 14th century comes from the Alps where the tree line fell by 70 to 300 meters. This observation is supported by the remains of peat deposits and forests at higher elevations than they presently occur. A similar 100-200 meter lowing of the tree line also occurred in Northern Germany.[48] It is apparent from the physical evidence gathered from every corner of Eurasia that the LIA affected at all of the areas later affected by the plague. Further evidence for the climatic change that heralded the start of the LIA can be found in historical records as well.

One such example is the Norse settlements Greenland and Iceland. In northern Greenland, there is archeological evidence of large Inuit villages that were developed for whaling and fishing. These Inuit settlements eventually were forced south around the start of the Little Ice Age until they came in contact with Viking colonies in southern Greenland. Conflict occurred over resources, and the Viking colonies eventually died out in the early 15th century, a fact attested to by contemporary ecclesiastical

---

[46] Xu, H., et al. 2002. "Temperature variations in the past 6000 years inferred from O^{18} of peat cellulose from Hongyuan, China." *Chinese Science Bulletin* **47**: 1578-1584. http://www.friendsofscience.org/documents/Solar%20Effects.html

[47] Naurzbaev, M.M. and Vaganov, E.A. 2000. "Variation of early summer and annual temperature in east Taymir and Putoran (Siberia) over the last two millennia inferred from tree rings." *Journal of Geophysical Research* **105**: 7317-7326. http://www.co2science.org/scripts/CO2ScienceB2C/subject/l/summaries/liarussia.jsp

[48] Lamb, *Climate, History, and the Modern World*, 436.

writings and the memoirs of the Vikings that later found the settlements abandoned.[49] Botanical evidence from the excavation of Viking colony sites in Greenland has shown the presence of grain pollen, which implies cultivation of this crop. Historical records predating the Little Ice Age also suggest that grain was grown in both Greenland and Iceland, an occupation not attempted again in this region until the present century[50] In Iceland, grain growing was given up in the 14th century, and in the late 15th century sea ice completely surrounded Iceland except for one port. Even from the highest mountains, it was difficult to spot open water. This resulted in the island getting its present name and is further evidence of the dramatic climate changes that were taking place at this time.[51]

Further historical evidence of the Little Ice Age comes from agricultural records, specifically viticulture. Emmanuel le Roy Ladurie notes that there were many "bad years" for wine during the LIA in France and surrounding countries due to very late harvests and very wet summers. Grapes were also grown in northern Germany at that time, an area which today cannot sustain commercial vineyards.[52] The cultivation of grapes was extensive throughout the southern portion of England from about 1100-1300. This area is about 400 miles farther north than the areas in France and Germany were viniculture is now practiced. At the time of the compilation of the *Domesday Book* by William the Conqueror in the late eleventh century, vineyards were recorded in 46 places in southern England, from East Anglia through to modern-day Somerset. In fact, Lamb suggests that during that period the amount of wine produced in England was substantial enough to provide significant economic competition with the producers in France. With the coming cooler climate in the

---

[49] Ibid., 248.

[50] Ibid., 257.

[51] Diamond, *Collapse*, 204.

[52] Ladurie, Emmanuel Le Roy. *Times of Feast, Times of Famine: A History of Climate Since the Year 1000*, (New York 1971), 97 [cited by Dr. Scott A. Mandia. " The Little Ice Age in Europe" http://www2.sunysuffolk.edu/mandias/lia/little_ice_age.html

1400's, temperatures became too cold for grape production and the vineyards in southern England gradually declined. German wine production also declined during the cooling experienced after the MWP and during the LIA. Between 1400 and 1700 German wine production was never above 53% of the production before 1300 and at times was as low as 20% of that production.[53] While it is obvious from ice cores, tree ring/ botanical data, and historical data that the Little Ice Age ushered in wetter, colder and stormier weather in Eurasia, the causative factors behind the shift are not well understood.

The Cause of the Little Ice Age

While it is relatively easy to find evidence for a general cooling trend in Eurasia following the Little Ice Age, it is more difficult to define the cause(s) for this phenomenon. Unlike the climatic anomaly that precipitated the first outbreak of the *Yersinia Pestis* plague which was most probably a volcanic event, the LIA would more than likely seem to be an amalgam of factors. The causes behind the Little Ice Age, whether global in extent or not, are not well understood. Four climate change mechanisms that operate on the time scale of centuries have been considered: volcanic eruptions, variations in solar energy, and changes in ocean circulation, and even anthropogenic influence. Although none of these on their own seem to reliably predict the observed climate changes throughout the Little Ice Age, a confluence of two or more of these phenomena could have conceivably brought about the LIA.

The idea of volcanism as a causative agent in global cooling is well established. It is known that ash and other small particulate matter injected into the stratosphere can effectively reduce incoming solar radiation received at the earth's surface. Sulfur compounds from eruptions condense into very tiny sulfuric acid droplets that form clouds which may

---

[53] Lamb, *Climate, History, and the Modern World,* 249

stay suspended in the stratosphere for years, further reducing incoming sunlight.[54] Ice core records indicate that the Little Ice Age was a time numerous volcanic eruptions: with an average of five major eruptions per century that equaled the intensity of the Krakatoa eruption in 1883. Such episodes would have injected massive quantities of micro particles and gases into the atmosphere. The ash content of two central Greenland ice cores, GISP 1 & 2, shows that the later years of the Medieval Warm Period from approximately 1100 to 1250 were quiet volcanically. Between 1250 and 1500, however, there were many eruptions at unknown locations in the northern hemisphere, most probably Iceland or the Aleutians due to the absence of corresponding cores in Antarctica.[55] Many scientists are sure that volcanic activity produced brief climatic extremes during the five cold centuries, but volcanism alone fails to explain the long purveyance of the LIA.

One factor that probably influenced the LIA and has yet to be proven conclusively is the apparent strong correlation between solar activity and global weather patterns. This theory was first proposed by E.W. Maunder, who "discovered the dearth of sunspots during a later period of the LIA, 1645-1715, and suggested that sunspots seem to be indicative of lower solar output and affect the amount of cosmic radiation reaching the Earth."[56] A 2001 study by Gerard Bond and his colleagues on "North Atlantic deep-sea sediment cores sought to find a temporal correlation with concentrations of the cosmogonic nuclides [nuclides formed by the collision of high energy solar radiation with an atom within the atmosphere of Earth]

---

[54] Pollock, J.B., et al., 1976, "Volcanic Explosions and Climatic Change: A Theoretical Assessment," Journal of Geophysical Research, 81:1071-1083. http://www.agu.org/pubs/

[55] Fagan, Brian. *Floods, Famines, and Emperors: El Niño and the Fate of Civilizations.* (New York: Basic Books, 1999), 224.

[56] "Maunder Minimum". Wikipedia – The Free Encyclopedia. 22 January 2007. http://en.wikipedia.org/wiki/Maunder_Minimum

Be^{10} (a beryllium isotope) and C^{14} (a carbon isotope), which can be used as proxies for solar activity."[57]

In this particular case, they utilized measurements of Be^{10} contained within the Greenland ice cap and C^{14} contained within Northern Hemispheric tree rings, demonstrating, in their words, that "over the last 12,000 years virtually every centennial time-scale increase in drift ice documented in our North Atlantic records was tied to a solar minimum." Hence, they concluded that the underlying climatic cycle of the LIA is solar-induced. Bond and his colleagues further concluded that "the solar-climate links implied by our record are so dominant over the last 12,000 years … it seems almost certain that the well-documented connection between the Maunder and Spörer [another solar epic occurring circa 1400-1570] solar minimums and the coldest decades of the LIA could not have been a coincidence," and that both the Little Ice Age and Medieval Warm Period "may have been partly or entirely linked to changes in solar irradiance."[58] While this theory cannot be conclusively proven, the evidence is certainly tantalizing. Another possible causative factor of the LIA and a new field of research by climate scientists involves the relationship between climate and changes in the ocean current conveyer belt system.

One of the most interesting and plausible factors for the Little Ice Age is the cumulative climatic effect of ocean currents and the atmospheric wind patterns. Both the global conveyer of ocean currents and the circulating atmospheric winds are responsible for bringing heat and moisture to the higher latitudes of the Earth.[59] Both short and long term climate in Eurasia are driven by changes in the surface temperature of the Atlantic Ocean and the flow of the Gulf stream. The Gulf Stream is essentially

---

[57] "The Little Ice Age" CO^2 Science. 21 April 2007 Center for the Study of Carbon Dioxide and Global Change. http://www.co2science.org/scripts/CO2ScienceB2C/subject/l/summaries/liaglobal.jsp

[58] Bond, et al. 2001. "Persistent solar influence on North Atlantic climate during the Holocene." *Science* **294**: 2130-2136. http://www.co2science.org/scripts/CO2ScienceB2C/articles/V4/N48/EDIT.jsp

[59] Lamb, *Climate, History, and the Modern World*, 23.

a gigantic river of warm tropical water flowing in the Atlantic. It moves vast amounts of energy in the form of heat and is responsible for making northern Eurasia habitable.[60] A decrease in surface temperature and/or a disruption of the Gulf Stream could have dramatic effects on the climate of Northwestern Eurasia. As warmer surface waters reach the colder northern waters, they begin to sink and carry atmospheric gas and salt with them. This subsidence effect influences creates a heat pump of sorts and helps regulate the continued regularity of ocean conveyer belt. Any slowdown in circulation of the conveyer leads to a drop in ocean temperatures.[61] Studies of coral, which like trees exhibit yearly growth bands, in the proximity of the Caribbean Gulf Stream corroborate the circulation slowdown and yielded C^{14} isotope data suggesting that mean water temperatures during the Little Ice Age did indeed decrease by about 1°C.[62] This temperature variation most probably fueled the atmospheric phenomena of the period and brought pronounced variations in Eurasian weather during the period.

The prevailing winds and storm patterns of the entire Atlantic and Western Eurasia are governed by a mechanism called the North Atlantic Oscillation (NAO), the northern equivalent of Southern Oscillation or El Nino. The NAO is the relationship between an area of high pressure over the Azores and an area of low pressure over Iceland. The relative pressure between these two determines the direction and intensity of tropical heat and storms in Europe.[63] A positive NAO, where there is a large pressure difference between the Azores and Greenland, on average can decrease rainfall in Europe by a little over an eighth of an inch per day and warm the air there by roughly 5 degrees Fahrenheit. A negative NAO, on the other hand, will increase rain to Eurasia as well as drop the temperatures

---

[60] Linden, *The Winds of Change*, 106-107.

[61] Fagan, *The Little Ice Age*, 26-28.

[62] Druffel, E. M. 1982. "Banded corals: changes in oceanic Carbon-14 during the little ice age." Science 218:13-19. Cited on and accessed via Druffel, E. M. 1982. "Banded corals: changes in oceanic Carbon-14 during the little ice age." Science 218:13-19. http://www.grisda.org/origins/10051.htm

[63] Linden, *The Winds of Change*, 173-174.

throughout Europe. Brian Fagan has surmised that the torrential downpours that heralded the onset of the LIA and caused the Great Famine of 1315-1322, directly resulted from a shift from a positive NAO to a negative NAO in the years 1312-1315.[64] Essentially, a disruption of ocean currents and a resultant change in ocean temperature are directly correlated to the NAO factor, which is known to bring cold, rainy weather when the pressure gradient is negative. Such an episode or several of them over time could certainly have precipitated the LIA.[65]

Another final theory put forward by William Ruddiman to explain the global cooling of the Little Ice Age involves gradual anthropogenic warming of the planet as the result of increased CO^2 that began with the rise of agriculture around 8,000 years ago. After taking into account possible natural causes for the greenhouse gas increases, Ruddiman speculates that early farmers clearing forests in Europe, India and China account for the surge of carbon dioxide, while rice paddies and burgeoning herds of livestock produced the extra methane. Ruddiman believes that a converse relationship exists between the sudden drop in CO^2 that corresponds to the LIA and the incidence of the Black Death. He notes that the Black Death depopulated Eurasia during those same centuries, such that fields and villages were abandoned and reclaimed by fast-growing forests that sucked carbon dioxide out of the atmosphere, resulting in the cooler temperatures felt worldwide.[66] Although provocative, Ruddiman's theory, unlike the preceding assertion by Fagan, fails to assess the weather anomalies that occurred in the decades before the outbreak of the plague.

64 Fagan, *The Little Ice Age*, 23-29.

65 Linden, *The Winds of Change*, 29.

66 Ruddiman, *Plows, Plagues, and Petroleum*, 139-146.

Did The Little Ice Age Create Conditions Ideal for the Black Death?

Clearly the Little Ice Age brought unprecedented climatic affects to Eurasia in the years immediately preceding the Black Death, as evidenced by the wealth of data cited above. As noted previously, the abrupt climate changes of the mid 530's precipitated a period of cool wet weather and led to a concatenation of climatic events that saw the rapid increase in the range of the rodents in whom the plague bacillus is endemic. In order to draw such a conclusion, one needs to assess the effects of

The Triumph of Death (Palermo) by Unknown Artist (c. 1446)

Did the cooler, wetter weather that began in the early 14th century create a similar scenario for the Black Death, which enabled it to migrate from one of its natural reservoirs in the eastern Eurasian Steppe to decimate one third to one half of Eurasia's population? In order to draw such a conclusion, one needs to assess the effects of prevailing weather patterns in Eurasia in the years before the Black Death. Since it is thought that the Black Death originated from an Asian locus, instead of an African reservoir as in Justinian's plague, any initial search must begin there. Since it is thought that the Black Death originated from an Asian locus, instead of an African reservoir as in Justinian's Plague, any initial search must begin there.

During the late 13th and early 14th centuries, the prevailing Eurasian wind patterns changed, perhaps due to a shift towards a more negative NAO. Europe, dominated by Atlantic breezes, became much wetter and cooler; by contrast, sirocco winds from the Sahara blew hot, dry air into the already arid region of central Asia.[67] Massive droughts spread through China during the early 1330's as evidenced by the chronicles of travelers like Marco Polo who traveled on the Silk Road.[68] The problems were exacerbated by heavy rains which caused cataclysmic flooding in which hundreds of thousands perished. In China, droughts and flooding decimated agricultural crop yields and to make matters worse swarms of locusts are recorded to have destroyed what crops were left. The resulting years of famine spanning from 1331 in the early 1340's claimed the lives of an estimated five million individuals according to court records.[69]

These occurrences caused Mongol horsemen to move their herds out of the Gobi Desert. At the same time the central Asian great gerbil, *Rhombomys opimus,* an endemic carrier of the plague living in Yunnan and the Manchurian steppe, also migrated towards the Gobi Desert and

---

67 Gottfried, Robert. *The Black Death.* (New York: Free Press, 1983), 34.

68 Linden, *The Winds of Change,* 80.

69 McNeil, *Plagues and People,* 162.

Mongolian grasslands in search of food and water, infecting local rodent populations with *Yersinia Pestis.*[70] From here it was only a matter of time until the bacillus was passed to rodents who cohabitate with human beings as their natural hosts died of drought and flooding. These set of circumstances are nearly ideal to those of the Justinian's Plague eight hundred years earlier; droughts followed by flooding leading to native foci displacement into areas with close human proximity.

The environmental calamities brought on by anomalous weather coinciding with the beginnings of the Little Ice Age gave rise to the first recorded outbreak of the Black Death in the Chinese province of Hubei in 1334, which claimed up to ninety percent of the population, an estimated five million people. During 1353–54, outbreaks in eight distinct areas throughout the Mongol-controlled China may have caused the death of two-thirds of China's population, often yielding an estimate of twenty-five million deaths. These figures are inferred from comparing the Chinese census of 1200 which counted approximately 123 million individuals to a 1393 census under the Ming Dynasty that revealed a population of approximately 65 million, a mortality approaching 50%.[71]

Just as in Justinian's Plague, ideal environmental conditions precipitated the plague eruption from generally isolated foci. In doing so, the *Rattus rattus* hosts of *Xenopsylla cheopis,* itself the host of the Yersinia *Pestis* bacilus, would follow the well-traveled Silk Road caravan route and the Mongol armies all the way across the continent as history repeated itself.

Clearly, movement by the Mongols and merchant caravans inadvertently brought the plague from central Asia to the Middle East and Europe. In fact, one vector of plague propagation involved Asian fur trappers picking up pelts of marmot that had died of the plague, skinning them, and selling the pelts (and their ravenous fleas) to traders who then took them to major centers of trade. The plague was reported in the trading cities of

[70] Fagan, *Floods, Famines, and Emperors*, 117.

[71] McNeil, *Plagues and People*, 173-175.

Constantinople and Trebizond in 1347. In that same year the Genoese possession of Kaffa, a seaport on the Crimean Peninsula in modern day Ukraine, came under siege by an army of Mongol warriors, backed by Venetian forces. In 1347, a terrible sickness began to strike the besieging army. According to accounts, so many died that the survivors had little time to bury them and bodies were stacked like cords of firewood against the city walls. Although the Mongol/Venetian alliance broke off the siege, the disease had already spread to the city. When the Genoese learned about the deaths in Kaffa, they attempted to quarantine all maritime traffic into Genoa, but the rats simply swam ashore and the great pandemic began.[72] The rapidity with which the plague spread into Europe is also linked to the preponderance of LIA climatic fluctuations were occurring both before and during the Black Death arrived in Genoa in 1347.

Between 1310 and 1330 Europe saw some of the worst and most sustained periods of bad weather in the entire Middle Ages, characterized by severe winters and rainy and cold summers, the causes of which have been speculated upon previously. The Great Famine of 1315-1322 resulted from the incessant rain and cold. The famine would smite most of western Eurasia from the Pyrenees to the Russian steppe and from Scottland to Italy.[73] Besides the flooding and intense gales that battered the continent, food shortages and skyrocketing prices were a fact of life during the Great Famine. Wheat, oats, and hay could not be harvested with any regularity for years and consequently livestock were unable to be fed and were butchered prematurely. The damp conditions gave raise to several outbreaks of typhoid throughout the period and in 1318 a pestilence of unknown origin, sometimes identified as anthrax, struck the malnourished animals of Europe. The disease targeted sheep and cattle, further reducing the food supply and income of the peasantry and stretching the fragile economy to brink of failure. It is estimated that

---

[72] Linden, *The Winds of Change*, 80-81.

[73] Lucas, Henry. "The Great European Famine of 1315, 1316, and 1317." *Speculum*, Vol. 5, No. 4 (Oct., 1930), 349. Accessed via JSTOR

between 10%–25% of the population of many cities and towns died. For the survivors, the net result of the Great Famine and the concomitant incidence of disease begot a mounting human vulnerability to epidemic disease due to weakened immunity.[74]

[74] Fagan, *Floods, Famines, and Emperors*, 28-40.

The Second Disappearance of the Plague

Justinian's Plague, after several waves of transference from city to city, region to region, around the Eurasian and African continents finally disappears from the historical record after raging for 210 years. One must assume that the chain of infection among rats, fleas, and humans abated because *Yersinia pestis* had failed to find an ecological niche where it could abide.[75] This was perhaps due to the steadily improving climate of the Medieval Warm Period. In comparison, The Black Death recurred in Europe and the Mediterranean for approximately four hundred years spanning the fourteenth to nineteenth centuries, although there were certainly intermittent periods of almost no activity. Although the retreat of the plague

Hand of God The Creation of Adam Sistine Chapel by Michelangelo Buonarroti (1509)

[75] Lamb, *Climate, History, and the Modern World*, 125. & McNeil, *Plagues and People*, 170.

from Europe was generally complete by the mid nineteenth century, the irregular and erratic nature of its second disappearance makes assigning causative events almost impossible.[76] Did climatic changes once again play a role in the disappearance of a mass killer?

The disappearance of major outbreaks of the plague during the late 17th century does not appear to have any environmental correlation, such as the probable link between end of Justinian's Plague and the Medieval Warm period. While the above research has elucidated the fact that beginnings of the Little Ice Age correspond nicely with the appearance of the Black Death, the end of the major plague outbreaks predates the accepted end of the Little Ice Age by at least two centuries. While some disagreement exists as to the definitive end of the LIA, the general consensus is that it did not end before 1850, nearly two centuries after the occurrence of the Great Plague of London.[77] A further problem with a causative climate change as it relates to end of the Black Death is evidenced by the fact that another mini-pandemic in China started at the beginning of the present warming period around 1850. This third pandemic paled in comparison to the previous two in terms of mortality and pervasiveness. Although this outbreak corresponded to a generally recognized warming trend, the time period was also associated with war and civil unrest within China.[78] Additionally, peasant farmers at this time were expanding agriculture into lands previously uncultivated, bringing man into direct contact with naturally occurring plague reservoirs.[79] Although the topic is not well researched, it does not appear that long term climatic changes brought about by asteroid impacts, solar radiance, and oceanic convection slow-downs ended the Black Death. It also appears unlikely that short term climate fluctuations such as NAO fluctuations, smaller volcanic events, or

---

[76] Slack, Paul. "The Disappearance of the Plague: An Alternative View", Economic History Review 34, 3 (1981) p.

[77] Fagan, *The Long Summer*, 249.

[78] McNeil, *Plagues and People*, 164.

[79] Ibid., 165.

anthropogenic CO^2 variances due to deforestation or agriculture played a part. The plague remains endemic in several areas of the world and small outbreaks have occurred often due to human encroachment upon infected rodent populations. No climatic correlation is needed to explain these incidences.

The notion that improved urban sanitation led to the demise of the Black Death does not take into account modern occurrences of the plague. Paul Slack champions the idea while brick buildings, sewer systems, and port quarantines did not actually halt the plague, these measure in some way mitigated its continued occurrence.[80] Although Slack's theory is logical, it theory also fails to recognize that the 1850 pandemic as well as subsequent outbreaks have occurred in urban areas with modern (at least by 17th century standards) sanitation practices. Such practices may mitigated some of the risk of another pandemic in modern times, but cannot be responsible for the disappearance of the Black Death in the 17th century. Clive Ponting also points out that humans living in urban areas may have gained a relative immunity over generations against the *Yersinia pestis* bacteria.[81] This hypothesis bears some credence as it has been posited that the CCR5-Delta 32 allele (gene variant) deletion mutation, which protects a relatively high percentage of Europeans from HIV infection, occurred due to strong selective pressure from a single event approximately seven hundred years ago, most probably the Black Death.[82]

Another possible theory favors an immunity vector in the carriers of the plague, not in humanity, in explaining subsidence of the Black Death in Europe. Andrew Appleby speculates that like humans, the carrier rats suffered massive die offs due to the plague and some were able to pass on

---

[80] Slack, Paul. "The Disappearance of the Plague: An Alternative View", Economic History Review 34, 3 (1981)

[81] Ponting, Clive. *A Green History of the World* (New York: Penguin Books, 1991), 227

[82] Kampis, Stephen. "The Black Plague, Its Ramifications, and the CCR5-Delta 32 Deletion Mutation" February 23, 2005. http://www.as.ua.edu/ant/bindon/ant475/Papers/Kampis.pdf

a relative immunity to their offspring.[83] Appleby also theorizes that the black rat (*Rattus rattus*) may have been exterminated and succeeded by the Norwegian, or brown rat (*Rattus norvegicus*). The brown rat, or sewer rat, lives in sewers as the name implies and generally, shuns contact with humans. In the late plague era, the brown rat was thus less prone to transmit the germ-bearing fleas to people if they contracted the bacillus and a population crash occurred.[84] Although Appleby does not suppose that these were the sole causative agents for the disappearance of the plague, he nonetheless gives them unequal weight when the evidence is sparse. It is probable that the environmental pressures of the LIA selected for the immunity of rats or even for the supplantation of the black rat by the brown, but only anecdotal evidence exists.

---

[83] Appleby, Andrew. "The Disappearance of the Plague: A Continuing Puzzle" *The Economic History Review*, New Series, Vol. 33, No. 2 (May, 1980),170-171 Accessed via JSTOR

[84] Ibid., 167.

Conclusion

There appears to be a strong correlation between sudden climatic shifts and the occurrence of the two great *Yersinia Pestis* plague pandemics. Justinian's Plague was preceded by the climate anomaly of 535-536, which darkened the skies worldwide for several years, ushered in an era of cool weather due to particulate matter in the atmosphere, and resulted in mass droughts followed by extensive flooding in most areas of Eurasia. A wealth of physical, literary, and anecdotal evidence strongly points to a gigantic volcanic eruption in the tropics, most probably in Indonesia. The weather anomalies that resulted disrupted the natural ecosystems of African rodents such as the gerbil within whom the plague bacillus found a natural host. The population crash and/or migration of these carriers brought them into contact with rodents who live in close proximity to man, such as *Rattus rattus*. Whether by necessity or opportunity, the plague was transmitted via the *Xenopsylla cheopis* flea to its new hosts. The fleas, unable to nourish themselves due to the plague bacilli multiplying in their stomach, ravenously jump from host to host in an effort to avoid starvation. *Rattus rattus*, *Xenopsylla cheopis*, and *Yersinia pestis* traveled along well used caravan routes in Egypt until arriving at the grain port of Alexandria. The rats and their deadly passengers were lured by copious amounts of food on board grain ships that ferried the plague off to every corner of the Roman world. After raging for 210 years, the plague disappeared from the pages of history. Another climatic shift, the Medieval Warm Period, coincided with the plague's disappearance. Positing that the plague occurred because ideal conditions caused by the climate anomalies resulting from the proposed eruption - droughts followed by wet and colder climate - one can logically assume that converse environmental conditions could theoretically aid in its diminution. This argument, while not a widely held view, provides a compelling clue to the otherwise inexplicable vanishing.

Causation also appears evident in the case of the beginning of the Little Ice Age and the incidence of the Black Death. The climatic vicissitudes that heralded the beginning of the LIA were very similar to the events that preceded Justinian's plague with the exception of sky darkening particulate matter: extremely cold weather, torrential rains, droughts, and massive flooding. Unlike the climate anomalies of 535-536, however, there is nothing close to an evidential smoking gun to link one event with the LIA. Various theories have been put forward to explain the occurrence of the LIA, and most are seen as probable contributors of the sudden climate change that occurred in Eurasia in the first four decades of the fourteenth century. In all likelihood, a confluence of several climatic drivers played a part in the climatic shift that immediately preceded the Black Death. Although the Black Death more than likely originated in an East Asian plague reservoir, the disruption of natural rodent ecosystems by dramatic weather events such as drought and flooding, mirrors that of Justinian's plague. Similarly, the unwitting partners in this plague's somewhat longer transmission sequence: *Rhombomys opimus, Marmota bobak, Rattus rattus, Xenopsylla cheopis,* and *Yersinia pestis* utilized the well-traveled Silk Road caravan route to migrate towards trading centers. Additionally, the conquering Mongol armies provided another opportunity for migration as they pushed west to conquer commercial centers like Genoese-controlled Kaffa. The bacillus was carried to Genoa and the rest of Europe from this Black Sea port. While the source of the Black Death seems to be strongly correlated to weather events associated with the LIA, no causal link relating to the prevailing climate of Eurasia can be identified as being associated with the end of the major Black Death outbreaks in the mid 17th century. Several theories ranging from urban sanitation, to genetic mutations, and rodent competition have been tendered to explain the end of the Black Death's 300 year reign of terror, but none appear plausible enough to have ended the plague on its own merit.

Bibliography

Appleby, Andrew. "The Disappearance of the Plague: A Continuing Puzzle" *The Economic History Review*, New Series, Vol. 33, No. 2 (May, 1980), 161-173. Accessed via JSTOR

Bond, G., Kromer, B., Beer, J., Muscheler, R., Evans, M.N., Showers, W., Hoffmann, S., Lotti- Bond, R., Hajdas, I. and Bonani, G. 2001. "Persistent solar influence on North Atlantic climate during the Holocene." *Science* **294**: 2130-2136. http://www.co2science.org/scripts/CO2ScienceB2C/articles/V4/N48/EDIT.jsp, Accessed April 27, 2007

Diamond, Jared. *Collapse: How Societies Choose to Succeed or Fail.* New York: Penguin Books; 2005

Epstein, Paul. "A Changing Climate for Disease and Death," *The Third World Network*, December 5, 2006. http://www.twnside.org.sg/title/twr125g.htm, Accessed November 3, 2007

Fagan, Brian. *Floods, Famines, and Emperors: El Niño and the Fate of Civilizations.* New York: Basic Books, 1999

Fagan, Brian. *The Long Summer; How Climate Changed Civilization.* New York: Basic Books, 2004

Fagan, Brian. *The Little Ice Age: How Climate Made History.* New York: Basic Books, 2005

Gottfried, Robert. *The Black Death.* New York: Free Press, 1983

Houghton, J. T., Ding, Y., Griggs, D. J., Noguer, M., Linden, P. J. Van Der, and Xiaosu, D. (eds) 2001, *Climate Change 2001: The Scientific Basis*, Intergovernmental Panel on Climate Change (IPCC), Cambridge University Press, Cambridge, UK. Accessed via www.grida.no/climate/ipcc_tar/wg1/070.htm, accessed April 27, 2007

Kampis, Stephen. "The Black Plague, Its Ramifications, and the CCR5-Delta 32 Deletion Mutation" February 23, 2005. Accessed via http://www.as.ua.edu/ant/bindon/ant475/Papers/Kampis.pdf, Accessed April 29, 2007

Karlen, Arno. Man and Microbes. New York: Simon & Schuster, 1995

Kavenaugh, Dan. "Specific Effect of Temperature Upon Transmission of the Plague Bacillus by the Oriental Rat Flea, *Xenopsylla Cheopis*" *The American Journal of Tropical Medicine and Hygiene Vol. 20* (1971): 264-273. http://www.ajtmh.org/cgi/content/abstract/20/2/264 Accessed November 2, 2007

Kelly, John. *The Great Mortality: An Intimate History of the Black Death, the Most Devastating Plague of All Time.* New York: Harper, 2005.

Keys, David. *Catastrophe: An Investigation Into the Origins of the Modern World.* New York: Ballantine Books, 1999

Ladurie, Emmanuel Le Roy. *Times of Feast, Times of Famine: A History of Climate Since the Year 1000*, New York: Doubleday, 1971

Lamb, H.H. *Climate, History and the Modern World.* London: Routledge; 1995

Linden, Eugene. *The Winds of Change: Climate, Weather, and the Destruction of Civilizations.* New York: Simon and Schuster, 2006

Little, Lester. *Plague and the End of Antiquity: The Pandemic of 541-750.* Cambridge University Press: Cambridge, 2007

Lucas, Henry. "The Great European Famine of 1315, 1316, and 1317." *Speculum*, Vol. 5, No. 4 (Oct., 1930), 343-377. Accessed via JSTOR

McNeil, William. *Plagues and People.* New York: Anchor Books, 1976

Naurzbaev, M.M. and Vaganov, E.A. 2000. "Variation of early summer and annual temperature in east Taymir and Putoran (Siberia) over the last two millennia inferred from tree rings." *Journal of Geophysical Research* **105**: 7317-7326. Accessed via http://www.co2science.org/scripts/CO2ScienceB2C/subject/l/summaries/liarussia.jsp, Accessed April 29, 2007

Nohl, Johannes. *The Black Death: A Chronicle of the Plague*. Yardley, PA: Westholme, 2006. Pearce, Fred. "Failing Ocean Current Raises Fears of a Mini Ice Age." NewScientist.com 30 November 2005 Accessed via http://www.newscientist.com/article.ns?id=dn8398, Accessed April 27, 2007

Pollock, J.B., et al., 1976, "Volcanic Explosions and Climatic Change: A Theoretical Assessment," Journal of Geophysical Research, 81:1071-1083. Accessed via http://www.agu.org/pubs/, Accessed August 8, 2007

Ponting, Clive. *A Green History of the World*. New York: Penguin Books, 1993

Porter, Roy. The Black Death. April 28, 2006. http://www.strath.ac.uk/Departments/History/barton/ds11.htm, Accessed April 30, 2007

Procopius, *History of the Wars*, 7 Vols., trans. H. B. Dewing, Loeb Library of the Greek and Roman Classics, (Cambridge, Mass.: Harvard University Press, 1914), Vol. I, pp. 451-473. http://www.fordham.edu/halsall/source/542procopius-plague.html, Accessed May 2, 2007

Ruddiman, William. *Plows, Plagues, and Petroleum: How Humans Took Control of Climate*. Princeton University Press: Princeton, 2005

Slack, Paul. "The Disappearance of the Plague: An Alternative View", Economic History Review 34, 3 (1981) 469-476. Accessed via JSTOR

Sutherland, William. *Days of Darkness (AD 535-AD 546)*. May 21, 2006. Ezinearticles.com. Accessed via http://ezinearticles.com/?Days-of-Darkness-(AD-535-AD-546)&id=202540, Accessed May 2, 2007

"The Volcano and Climate Model" Earth Bulletins ©2004-2007 Updated April 29, 2007. The American Museum of Natural History. http://earthbulletin.amnh.org/D/3/2/, Accessed May 1, 2007

"The Little Ice Age" CO^2 Science . 21 April 2007 (last updated) Center for the Study of Carbon Dioxide and Global Change. http://www.co2science.org/scripts/CO2ScienceB2C/subject/l/summaries/liaglobal.jsp, Accessed April 29, 2007

Richard D. Tkachuck "The Little Ice Age" Geoscience Research Institute ©1983 http://www.grisda.org/origins/10051.htm, Accessed April 29, 2007

Wohletz, KH, 2000, *Were the Dark Ages triggered by volcano-related climate changes in the 6th century?* Los Alamos National Laboratory. http://www.ees1.lanl.gov/Wohletz/Krakatau.htmed Accessed April 25, 2007

Xu, H., Hong, Y., Lin, Q., Hong, B., Jiang, H. and Zhu, Y. 2002. "Temperature variations in the past 6000 years inferred from O^{18} of peat cellulose from Hongyuan, China." *Chinese Science Bulletin* **47**: 1578-1584. http://www.friendsofscience.org/documents/Solar%20Effects.html, Accessed April 29, 2007

About the Author

R. Christian Bilich is a professional consultant and amateur researcher. His research interests include environmental history, paleo-archeology, biblical archeology, history of religion, and economic history, and classical studies.

www.ingramcontent.com/pod-product-compliance
Lightning Source LLC
La Vergne TN
LVHW051021080826
845145LV00009B/2734

* 9 7 8 1 7 3 6 8 7 0 6 0 0 *